The Nature Club
The Everywhere Bear

D1016451

This book is a work of fiction.

Text copyright © 2019 by Rachel Mazur
Cover illustrations copyright © 2019 by Elettra Cudignotto
Inside illustrations copyright © 2019 by Rachelle Dyer
Edited by Emma Irving and Julie Mazur Tribe

A portion of the proceeds from the sale of this book will benefit black bear conservation.

Library of Congress Cataloging-in-Publication Data is available upon request.
ISBN 978-1-7329156-2-6 (paperback)
ISBN 978-1-7329156-7-1 (ebook)

First edition 2019

10 9 8 7 6 5 4 3 2 1

Wild Bear Press operates on the simple premise that nature-based stories connect children with the natural world and inspire them to protect it.

Visit us on the Web! www.natureclubbooks.com

The Nature Club
The Everywhere Bear

Rachel Mazur

WILD BEAR PRESS

For Sydney and Spencer, who
bring the sparkle and the fun

1

Brooke laughed as she jumped from log to log, her dark, curly hair bouncing as she went. She wanted to reach the edge of the creek without touching the ground, which was muddy from last night's rain. For some reason, the logs looked blurry to her, so each time she jumped, she had to rely on a bit of luck. It was working well until her last jump—when she landed on something slippery and fell on her butt in the muck. "Gross," she groaned, realizing she had slid right through a pile of animal poop.

Brooke stood up and looked down at her mud-stained purple shorts. As she examined the mess, she noticed a set of tracks in the mud. Squinting to look at them, she first thought they were from a human. There were tracks that looked like they were made from human hands, and others that looked like they were made from human feet.

Then she bent over to study them and saw that, on the tracks of the feet, the toes were all long and the big one pointed outward.

So it couldn't be a human, Brooke thought. *But what are they from? What walks on all fours and has big toes that look more like thumbs?* She considered it for a bit and finally snapped her fingers. *They must be from a monkey*, she thought.

At that moment, her best friends, Izzy and Tai, walked up and with a simple, "Hi Brooke," made her jump.

"Oh, hi," she replied while continuing to study the tracks.

"What are you looking at, and why are you so muddy?" Izzy asked, looking at the mud splattered all over Brooke's legs. "You even have mud up on your purple headband."

"Hey, ignore the mud for a second. I found some monkey tracks over here," Brooke replied. Izzy and Tai glanced at each other and burst out laughing.

"You found *what*?" Izzy asked while eyeing Tai

with a smile.

"You heard her," grinned Tai, tipping his tan cowboy hat toward the tracks. "She found tracks from the little-known American monkey."

"Brooke, there are no monkeys in the United States. Unless one escaped from a zoo," Izzy said between giggles.

Brooke frowned and straightened up. "You're just jealous you didn't find them," she said.

"Right," Tai said. "Let's take a look." Tai and Izzy surrounded Brooke to look at the tracks.

"They do look like monkey tracks," Izzy observed.

Tai gave Izzy a sideways glance. "Now I think you're both crazy," he said.

"Well then, what are they from?" Brooke challenged.

"I don't know," Tai replied.

"Let's find out," Izzy suggested. "I'll go get the mammal track guidebook and be right back." Then she ran off toward the house her family was renting for the summer, which was right near

Green County Park.

While Izzy was gone, Tai asked, "How did you come up with a monkey?"

"I'll tell you if you promise to stop laughing," Brooke responded with her hands on her hips.

"I promise to stop laughing," Tai said, trying to keep a straight face.

"Okay. Since the tracks look human, but the big toe looks more like a thumb, they have to be from a monkey," Brooke explained.

"I know how we can find out for sure," Izzy said after returning with a ruler, a camera, and her guidebook on local animals' tracks.

"Let's measure the tracks and compare them with what the book shows," Izzy said.

"And then," Tai added with a smile, "we'll see if we still come up with a monkey."

Brooke rolled her eyes and pulled a half-eaten Astro Bar out of her pocket.

"Hey! Next time, bring some of those bars for us, too," Tai said.

"I got a box of these candy bars last week from

a neighbor and I can't stop eating them. They are delicious. I'd give you one—but they are only for monkey trackers."

"Oh, come on," Tai pleaded. "I'll track a whole troupe of monkeys with you."

"Too late. It was my last one," Brooke smiled and popped the last piece into her mouth.

"Hey, chocolate lovers. Are you ready to get to work?" Izzy asked.

"Sure thing, President Izzy," Tai joked. Izzy, who was the president of their Nature Club despite her shy personality, blushed and handed him the measuring tape. Then she pulled her straight brown hair into her standard ponytail to get started.

Together, they measured the length and width of each print and the length and width of the distance between the prints. They also took note of the gait—the pattern of steps and how they fell in relation to each other.

Tai then took a few photos while Izzy flipped through the book. Brooke tried to follow along by peering over Izzy's shoulder, but the words on the pages looked blurry from where she stood.

"Let's see," Izzy said as she flipped through the book. "The larger tracks are almost four inches long, so we can rule out all the little critters, like mice, squirrels, and chipmunks.

"And there are a bunch of things it obviously isn't—like a deer or a rabbit or a coyote.

"It looks kind of like an opossum," she continued, "but the tracks are larger, and their gait is different. And it looks kind of like a river otter, but it's—"

"Stop telling us what it isn't. Just tell us what it is," Brooke pleaded.

Izzy looked at Brooke crossly for a moment and then turned back to flipping through the book. Finally, she yelled, "Aha! There's your monkey!"

Tai leaned over Izzy to look at the book. "You're right, Izzy. The tracks match." Pointing to some text under the photo of the track, he added, "Even the habitat is right. It says, 'Raccoon tracks are often found near water.'"

"Are you sure?" Brooke asked.

"Sorry, Brooke. It's lookin' like today's not the day you become famous," Tai said. "But raccoons are cool, too. Right?"

"Right," Brooke sighed.

"Hey, look," Izzy added, "on the next page there's a picture of raccoon scat." Noticing Brooke's confused look, Izzy explained, "You know, poop. Scat is animal poop. If we had some scat, we could be even more sure we're right."

Brooke sighed. "Well, actually, we might," she said, running her fingers through her thick, curly, dark hair.

"Where?" Izzy asked.

"On top of that log right there," Brooke said, pointing. "I accidentally stepped in it when I jumped on the log. I slid through it and fell in the mud." She turned around and showed her friends the big muddy spot on the back of her shorts.

Tai and Izzy burst into another round of laughter as they made their way to the log to examine what was left of the scat. Although it was squished, it did look like the scat in the picture.

Brooke now also laughed. "I guess a monkey was a bit of a stretch for this habitat."

"Let's see if we can figure out what the raccoon was doing," Izzy suggested.

"Great idea," Tai said. He backed up to look at the entire set of tracks. "Watch where you walk," he added, careful to not step on the prints.

From a bit of a distance, it was easier to investigate where the tracks came from and where they went. It looked as if the raccoon had entered the beach from the nearby bushes, walked straight to the water, and then walked back to the bushes. From there, the tracks disappeared.

Brooke called to Izzy. "Can you read what raccoons do in water?"

Izzy, who was still looking at the tracks, said, "Can you do it? The book is in your backpack. I stuck it in there so it wouldn't get muddy." After a dramatic pause, she added, "Not that there was much room in your bag with all the Astro Bar wrappers in there."

Brooke mumbled something about not cleaning out her backpack for a while and then went to retrieve the book. She opened it and found the raccoon page, but the words looked blurry and she could barely make them out. Handing the book to Izzy, she said, "Come on, you're the bookworm. You read it."

Izzy stood up and looked at Brooke sideways, but then she took the book and scanned the page. "Raccoons are omnivores and will eat almost anything that comes their way," she read. "If they're near water, they will wet their food before eating it."

"Well, isn't that polite of them?" Brooke observed.

"Actually," Izzy responded, "they don't wet their food to wash it. It says here they wet it 'to increase the sensitivity of their paws to feel and identify their food.'"

With that mystery solved, the kids hung out at

the creek and sketched in their journals until Izzy said, "I'd better go get my little brother, Zack, from my Grandma Pearl's house."

"I'd better get going, too," Brooke said. "I told my dad I'd help make dinner."

"Ditto," Tai said. "I want to get home and ride my horse, Dune, before dark."

As always since forming the Nature Club, the friends spent time picking up trash before leaving. They had sponsored a community trash pickup day right there at Green County Park just the month before, so it should have been clean. But it was a mess! Strangely, the biggest mess came from behind the bush, the same spot where the raccoon tracks emerged.

"That poor raccoon is hanging out in a mess," Izzy observed.

"A gross mess," Brooke agreed. "Hey, look," she said, pointing to an Astro Bar wrapper in the bush. "At least the litterbug has good taste in candy bars."

"Too bad someone already ate that one, too,"

Tai groaned. "It wasn't you, was it?"

"Are you accusing me of littering?" Brooke asked, her eyes wide open.

"Maybe . . . ." Tai looked at Brooke's horrified expression. "Oops. I guess not. Sorry."

"Grrrrr!" Brooke replied.

"Okay, you two, we're all friends here. Let's get to work," Izzy said. The three of them worked until the bulk of the mess was bagged up and stuffed into the park's dumpster. Then the friends spent some time making notes about what they saw and sketching the tracks in their journals before parting for the evening. Tai retrieved his bike to pedal home while Brooke and Izzy left together. After they said goodbye at Izzy's house, Brooke continued to the end of the road where she lived with her mom and dad.

2

When Brooke stepped inside her house, she found her dad, Mr. Clark, in the kitchen making a salad.

He smiled at her and shook his head. "Wow. You are a mess. Why don't you go change and then wash your hands and help me out?" he suggested.

Brooke nodded and put down her backpack. She silently left the room and then reappeared in clean clothes. Slowly, she turned on the sink and soaped up. While rinsing her hands, her dog, Blue, came running in from outside to stand next to her. When even that didn't make her smile, Mr. Clark handed her a towel. "Everything okay?" he asked his normally loud and energetic daughter.

Brooke squinted at the blurry words on the soap dispenser. "Yes, fine," she answered quietly.

Her dad, hoping for a conversation, tried again. "Anything interesting at the creek today?"

Brooke smiled. "Actually, yes. I found animal tracks. Izzy and Tai helped me figure out they were from a raccoon. I didn't even know there were raccoons around here."

Mr. Clark laughed. "That's because those sneaky little critters are only out at night," he said. "That's when they eat the eggs of the birds you love so much."

"They do?" Brooke asked, her eyes wide.

"Oh, yes," he assured her. He handed her a carrot, then listed all of Brooke's beloved animals that raccoons eat—including frogs, turtles, and even rabbits—while they finished chopping vegetables. "How'd you figure out it was a raccoon?" he asked.

Brooke pulled out the track book Izzy had accidentally left in Brooke's backpack. She explained how they had taken measurements and compared what they had found with tracks shown in the book. "Only . . . ," she said, and stopped.

"What is it, honey?" her dad asked gently.

"Only I couldn't read the words," Brooke blurted out, an anguished look on her face.

"Oh, Brooke," he said reassuringly. "There are probably lots of words in that book I don't know either. Ecology has its own language. You just have to get familiar with it."

"No, Dad," Brooke said, tears streaming down her face. "It isn't that I couldn't understand the words. I couldn't even make out the letters. They were blurry. Am I losing my eyesight?"

"Let's see," he replied, opening the book to the page on raccoons. "Can you read anything written on this page?"

Brooke hesitated before looking. "I can see the title fine, but all the other words are blurry."

"Can you make out any of them?"

"I can read, 'Raccoons eat almost anything,' but I can't read the next word."

"The next word is 'including.' Maybe you just blocked out the word 'including' because after that it says 'birds' eggs,'" Mr. Clark teased, trying to make her laugh. It didn't work. Instead, she talked about all the trash they had found in the bushes at the park.

"Funny," her dad replied. "Mrs. Green down the street said an animal had gotten into her trash and some of the other neighbors' trash recently and made a huge mess. I wonder if it's related?" He paused and then changed the subject. "Come on, let's put some chicken on the grill. I'll call tomorrow to make you an appointment to get your eyes checked."

Brooke started to follow her dad into the backyard but paused to quickly duck into her room and sneak a few bites of an Astro Bar. When she caught up with him outside, she helped him place chicken and onions on the grill and then watched while he slathered them with homemade barbecue sauce. Usually just the smell of that sauce would make Brooke smile, but today, she couldn't muster up an appetite.

A few moments later, Brooke's mom, Mrs.

Clark, arrived home from work. She joined them with a tray of drinks. "Everything okay?" she asked Brooke, sensing something was awry when her normally bubbly daughter hardly looked up. Brooke fiddled with her drink while her father briefed her mother on the raccoon tracks and Brooke's need for an eye appointment.

"I'm not surprised," said Mrs. Clark. "I was about your age when I first got glasses."

Brooke turned to her mother. "You had glasses?"

"For most of my life—I was blind as a bat without them."

"But I've never seen you wearing glasses."

"When you were three years old, I had surgery to repair my eyesight. Before that, I wore them all the time. I was hoping you wouldn't inherit my bad eyesight, but perhaps you did. At least it's solvable."

"Why couldn't I inherit Dad's eyesight?"

"Oh, come on, there are lots of worse things that can happen to you. Maybe to inherit my good looks you also had to inherit my eyesight," Mrs. Clark joked, attempting to lighten Brooke's mood. Brooke groaned. "Lots of people wear glasses or contact lenses," her mother continued. "What are you so worried about?"

"Softball."

"Softball?"

"Yes, softball. I love it and I want to keep playing."

"Reggie Jackson wore glasses when he played baseball," her dad interjected. "If anything, wearing glasses will make you a better ball player because you'll be able to see the ball more clearly."

"What about the way they look? You know how much I love to wear fun, colorful outfits— especially purple ones. Glasses are so boring."

"You, my darling daughter, could never be boring!"

While Brooke and her mom continued talking, Mr. Clark fed Blue on the back porch and set the outdoor table. "Time to eat!" he called.

Brooke and her mother joined him at the table. "Now, tell me about those raccoon tracks," Mrs. Clark said.

Brooke, feeling moody, described the event without enthusiasm while her parents ate and then mumbled something about clearing the table. As she stacked the dishes, she pretended she wanted to give her parents a chance to relax, but in reality, she didn't want them to notice she had hardly eaten. Her bad mood had taken away the little appetite she'd had left after filling up on candy bars. Plus, while Brooke adored her parents, there were times when she just wanted to be alone.

As she washed the dishes under the kitchen window, she heard her father say, "I love this time of night." And even though he said this almost every night, her mother replied, "Me, too," as if hearing it for the first time. Brooke looked out the window and smiled when she saw her parents holding hands as they watched the sunset.

With the kitchen cleaned, Brooke decided to

take the trash out before going to bed. She normally got up early to bring the trash to the curb the morning before pickup and then went back to bed for a few more hours of sleep, but lately, she'd been having trouble getting up. After collecting all the trash in the house, she carried it outside, loaded it into the big outdoor can, and rolled it to the curb. On the way back in, she said good night to her parents and called to Blue, who ran over and followed her into the house.

In her room, Brooke sent her brother a long email. He was older and had been away in the military for the past three years, but he always took time to write Brooke back and give her advice. She squinted as she looked at the screen, even after making the font huge so she could see what she was writing.

After hitting "send," Brooke picked up a book to read in bed, but even the title looked blurry, so she put it back down. Instead, she curled up with Blue and daydreamed about the events of the day before falling into a deep sleep.

3

As Brooke slept, animals stirred just outside her window. Under the light of a crescent moon, bats used echolocation to forage for juicy insects while a fox silently stalked a rabbit whose luck was about to run out. A great horned owl hooted to its mate from high in a tree, and field mice scurried about below, unaware of the danger perched above them. A bobcat walked about, looking for prey as if he owned the night, and all the while the crickets chirped.

Nearby, just beyond the Clarks' yard, where the neighborhood became forest, a mama bear rose from her day bed, awakening her two cubs as she stood. Normally, she was active during the day, but the week before she'd found a new food source she could only access at night. It was right in the middle of the neighborhood, an area she used to avoid since she feared humans and their cars and noise.

Last week, however, the scents coming from the neighborhood were stronger and much too tempting to resist. She finally left the safety of the forest to explore. The strongest scents came from open kitchen windows, but she wasn't yet ready to enter buildings. Luckily, other smells came from large plastic containers sitting by themselves on the curb. She approached one cautiously and then tipped it over. *Bingo!* She feasted on the contents before returning to find her cubs.

With the memory of last week's food still strong in her mind, the mama bear decided to patrol the neighborhood again tonight. She chased her cubs up a tree to keep them safe and, using grunts and clicks, told them to stay put. Then she followed her nose and relied on her memory to look for food.

First, she came upon a warm grill that had just enough barbecue sauce crusted onto it to smell delicious. She sniffed around and found a piece of meat that had fallen into the grass. Nearby, she found a scattering of sunflower seeds that had fallen from a bird feeder in the tree above. She nibbled on the seeds and then stood up and sniffed the air for more food.

The mama bear then followed her nose to the same type of plastic container she'd found the previous week. She knocked it over with one push and devoured the contents. Sniffing and exploring, she learned there was one of these at every house!

She took the best bits of food from each one before moving on to the next. She did this for about two hours, stopping only after she was too full to eat any more. She then returned to her cubs, using grunts and clicks to tell them to come back down. Once they were back together, they settled down near the edge of the forest to sleep.

Another resident of the night was slower to get started. From deep within a cavity in an oak tree outside the Clarks' house, a raccoon hesitated before leaving her den. She knew larger animals were around and wanted to keep her young ones safe, but she also had to feed them—and they were hungry. So, finally, as the moon rose higher in the sky, she tentatively stuck her nose out of the den to sniff the night air before emerging and jumping onto the ground. Her three kits, sometimes called cubs like the little bears, followed, each with a characteristic black mask and striped tail.

As the kits watched and copied her, the mother raccoon started to sniff and rub her paws on the ground, searching for earthworms to crush and devour. The ground was wet, so the rewards were good that night, and the whole family ate its fill.

But soon she was drawn to a stronger scent, one coming from behind the house that sat near her den tree. With her kits following, she sniffed her way to the back of the house and explored until she, too, came upon a large metal grill. It was warm and definitely inedible but had a delicious flavor when she licked it.

Rewarded by taste but still hungry for food, the mother stood up to sniff the air. A bouquet of scents once again filled her nose. She moved toward the smell while repeatedly stopping to sniff the air and paw at the ground. Soon she found that same large plastic container, now conveniently dumped on its side for her and her kits to enter. She approached it hesitantly at first and then climbed in with all three kits.

The family ate what it could and then emerged to search for more food. Following their noses, they, too, found one of those large plastic containers at every single house on the block—each one conveniently lying on its side. The mother raccoon—aware there was also the scent of a bear at each container—stayed vigilant as the kits explored. After her family ate its fill, she led the kits back to the safety of their den.

By the time the mother raccoon finally fell asleep just before dawn, she, like the mama bear before her, had learned of a whole new source of food for her family—food that was easier to get, tastier, and more filling than anything she had ever eaten before.

4

When Brooke woke the next morning, her father was already in his favorite chair in the living room, drinking coffee. He greeted her with a cheerful, "Good morning, honey."

"Where's Mom?" she replied.

"What about, 'Hi, Dad?'" he complained.

"Oh, sorry Dad," Brooke laughed. She gave him a kiss on the cheek. "Hi, Dad. Where's Mom?"

Mr. Clark rolled his eyes and smiled. "She had an early shift at the hospital. She's already been gone for two hours. Why don't you sit down and drink some coffee with me?"

"You know I don't drink coffee," Brooke giggled. She grabbed a glass of milk and sat down with him.

"What's on the agenda for today?" he asked. Mr. Clark taught graphic design at the local college, so he had summers off and often spent his days chaperoning Brooke and her friends on their many adventures.

"Actually, nothing," she replied. "Izzy is spending the day working in her Grandma Pearl's garden, and Tai is helping his dad clean out their garage."

"Sounds like family chore day. I like it. How about you spend the day doing chores with me?" he suggested. "We can start by bringing the trash can in from the curb."

Brooke pretended to think it over. "Hmmm. I will, but only if we can have pancakes with syrup first," she teased.

"It's a deal," he said and got to work in the kitchen.

The truth was, Brooke loved chore days with her dad. These days always involved interesting outdoor projects and ice cream sundaes.

After finishing breakfast and cleaning up the dishes, Brooke checked her email and happily found a response from her brother. She enlarged the font to read it. He told her all about his adventures and ended with some advice for her. He wrote, "I'm so sorry about the tough times and wish I was there to help, but I believe in you. I bet the solution is easier than you think, but even if it isn't, stay on course and believe in yourself."

Brooke smiled but wondered what the easy solution was. She then sneaked a bite of an Astro Bar before joining her dad to retrieve the trash can. When they got there, they were met with a surprise. Instead of sitting empty on the curb, the can had been knocked over, and trash was strewn everywhere.

"What a mess!" Brooke exclaimed.

"What happened here?" her father asked.

"I don't know. I took the trash out last night so I wouldn't have to get up early this morning," answered Brooke.

"Was it windy last night?" her father asked.

"A little, but . . ." Brooke's voice trailed off.

"Not enough to make this mess," Mr. Clark finished her thought. "So, what did?"

Together they righted the can and immediately noticed tracks on it—tracks unmistakably from a raccoon.

"I guess raccoons really do eat anything—even from the trash. And they must be stronger than they look," Mr. Clark observed. "I wonder if it was also raccoons that got into Mrs. Green's trash at least two times last week?"

"Gross," Brooke commented while rubbing on a stomach cramp she had gotten from eating the candy bar too quickly. She then looked up and noticed a trail of trash heading toward Green County Park. Thinking of the Astro Bar wrapper she'd found at the park, she lamented, "Oh no. The trash at the creek might *have* been from our house. The raccoon could have dragged it over there from here."

"Well, let's not let a raccoon spread any more of our garbage around," her dad said as he began picking up the mess.

Brooke joined him. "Even if they do reach thirty pounds, how would a raccoon be strong enough to flip this thing?" she asked.

"I don't know, but I'd sure like to see," he responded.

They stood quietly, thinking to themselves for a few minutes, when Brooke exclaimed, "We need to have a stakeout!"

"A what?" Mr. Clark asked.

"A stakeout! We could put out the trash and then camp in the backyard and watch to see what happens!"

"Excellent idea. Let's do it on the next garbage night," Mr. Clark said, catching Brooke's excitement.

"Really?" Brooke asked, wide-eyed. "Can Izzy and Tai come? And Izzy's little brother, Zack?"

"Of course. We'll need their help. Until then, we will keep this can locked up in the garage."

After cleaning up the mess, they spent the rest of the day fixing their greenhouse. One whole wall had collapsed over the winter. The work was hard, but they had a lot of fun together. Brooke's dad even let her use the cordless drill.

When they put in the last screw, Mr. Clark said, "I think we're done. You know what it's time for, right?"

"Ice cream sundaes!" they yelled in unison.

Mr. Clark put away his tools while Brooke grabbed their bike helmets and sneaked another bite of an Astro Bar. She made a quick stop in the bathroom to pick at a pimple she'd found on her chin and then ran back outside.

In no time, they were on their bikes and on their way. Last year, Brooke would make the trip easily, but today she felt winded and could barely keep up with her father. As they rode, they saw trash strewn all over the streets and a few other cans tipped over.

"Wow, that raccoon really made the rounds," Brooke remarked. "Or maybe it has a lot of friends. I guess ours wasn't the only house to get hit last night."

"You know, Brooke," Mr. Clark remarked, "we've seen so much trash today it's made me want to have a zero-waste snack. What do you say we get cones instead of cups?"

"I'm in."

Brooke got mint chocolate chip on a cake cone and her dad got mocha almond fudge on a sugar cone. It had been a great day.

They rode in silence for a few blocks before Mr. Clark spoke again. "I could really go for some of your mother's olive and spinach pizza."

"Me too," Brooke agreed.

When they arrived home, Mrs. Clark was already there, raving about the greenhouse. "I just love it. Thank you both for your hard work. I decided to thank you by surprising you with homemade pizza."

Brooke smiled with gratitude while Mr. Clark observed, "Great minds think alike."

5

The following Thursday afternoon, it was time to set up for the stakeout. Mr. Clark hummed cheerfully as he went into the garage to get out their big family tent. He carried the tent into the backyard and called to Brooke to help him find a good spot, "Where should we set up the tent?"

Brooke, who was rushing to fill up the bird feeder with sunflower seeds and, in her haste, spilling seeds all over, called back to him, "How about in the back corner?"

"Sounds good to me," he said, pulling the tent out of the bag.

Brooke quickly put the top back on the bird feeder and walked over to help. As usual, Brooke and her dad had to remember how to put the tent together. After several false starts, they had it standing. "Let's try to remember how we did it so it's easier next time," Mr. Clark suggested.

"Right," Brooke said, looking at him sideways. "That usually works well for us." They broke into laughter realizing they had set that same tent up dozens of times and never seemed to remember how to do it.

"Anybody home?" came a holler from around the garage.

"We're back here," Brooke called, recognizing Tai's voice.

"Awesome!" Tai exclaimed as he rounded the garage and saw the tent all set up. "Can I help?"

"Sure thing," Mr. Clark responded. "How about using those healthy lungs of yours to blow up the air mattresses?"

"You got it, sir!"

As Tai blew up the air mattresses, Brooke wheeled the trash can out of the garage and set it in full view of the tent. Then Brooke and Tai filled the tent with pillows, sleeping bags, and flashlights.

Satisfied, Mr. Clark said, "Time for a

barbecue."

"Are we going to have your special barbecue sauce, Mr. Clark?" Tai asked.

"Absolutely! And today, Brooke will do the honors of spreading it thick on the chicken."

Brooke, knowing this was a job her father rarely shared, was honored. The only problem was that as it got darker, she had a harder and harder time seeing what she was doing and accidentally put on way too much sauce. *Oh well*, she thought. *Hopefully if some sauce is good, more is better.*

By the time the chicken was done, the sauce had not only dripped all over the chicken, but all over the grill, too. Brooke removed the chicken with tongs onto a big serving plate, unintentionally leaving some chunks behind that had gotten stuck to the grill in the sticky sauce.

Mr. and Mrs. Clark set up the outdoor table with Tai's help, and then the group gorged on the chicken, plus their favorite side dishes of fresh salad and corn on the cob.

When they were done, they loaded all the trash into the outdoor can to use it as a lure for the raccoon.

Izzy showed up right after they finished cleaning up from dinner. She had brought Zack, who was grinning and balancing a large container on top of his bright red hair.

"Are you kids hungry? We ate barbecued chicken and we have leftovers," Mrs. Clark said.

"Thank you, but I'm a vegetarian," Izzy said.

"The chicken was raised locally *and* ranged freely," Brooke said. "Are you sure?"

"Sorry, but I just can't eat an animal. Animals have rights, too," Izzy said.

"I'm not a vegetarian," Zack said, glancing around for the chicken. "I'll eat it."

"But we both already ate," Izzy reminded him.

"If you both already ate, what's in that big container Zack has on his head?" Tai asked.

Zack smiled. "Cookies!"

"We just made them," Izzy said. "There's enough for everyone to have two."

37

In just moments, the group gobbled them up.

"Delicious!" Mrs. Clark said.

"I could eat at least ten more," Tai announced, picking at the crumbs.

"Hmm," Izzy mused. "There were fifteen cookies. My mom and Cody each had one before I left the house, so I brought thirteen here—but there are only six of us."

"That means someone had three," Tai chimed in. "Who's guilty?" He looked around, but no one would own up to taking an extra cookie.

"Well," Mrs. Clark said, changing the subject, "I've got another early shift at the hospital so I'm going to sleep inside tonight, but wake me up if anything exciting happens. I'll keep Blue with me so he doesn't scare your raccoon away and ruin all the fun." She called to Blue, who got up and then followed her inside.

At that point, the cookie sugar kicked in and everyone got excited about the night ahead.

"I can't wait to see a wild monkey," Tai teased.

Brooke laughed. "I'm going to see that

raccoon-shaped monkey if it takes all night."

Even Mr. Clark was excited. "It isn't every night I get to camp in the wilds," he said. He started making crazy wild animal sounds and soon everyone joined in.

The group all vowed they would stay awake all through the night to see the raccoon.

They started strong, eating popcorn and telling jokes. But as it got later, they fell asleep, one by one, until only Brooke was awake.

Having sneaked the missing cookie, she was extra sugared, totally excited, and alert. For a while, she sat up waiting, peeking outside whenever she heard any little sound. Once the moon rose, she didn't even need a flashlight to make out shapes.

When Brooke became bored of sitting, she lay down with just her head sticking out of the tent. She noticed she had left Blue's dog food dish out, and he hadn't finished his food. She thought about getting up and putting it away, but by then she was in a post-sugar crash and couldn't motivate herself to do it. Instead, she finally put down her head and closed her eyes.

6

As Brooke dozed off, a mama bear stretched to wake up. She sent her cubs up a tree and then sniffed the air before heading off to feed from the plastic containers in the neighborhood. Tonight, the sweet scent of barbecue sauce was stronger than ever. She made her way directly to the Clarks' grill and, although it was still warm, started eating the chunks of meat left on it.

She focused on the meal in front of her, not knowing that a mother raccoon and her kits were waiting to take their own turn at the grill. When she finished the scraps of meat, she turned to search for the next source of food, knocking the grill lid to the ground as she moved away.

7

Crash! The sound of clanking metal startled Brooke awake. She looked up and tried to make out the raccoon in the dark. Only the animal before her was much too big to be a raccoon. Then what was it? Brooke squinted to get a better look and realized: *It was a . . . bear!*

Brooke tried to alert the others, but when she opened her mouth to yell, no sound came out. Her mouth just hung wide open as she watched the bear finish licking the grill and then bend down to eat the last of Blue's dinner from his doggie bowl.

The furry beast then turned, sniffed the air, and started walking toward the tent. Brooke froze! Her eyes grew as big as saucers as she watched the bear approach. Her mind raced. *Should I warn the others? What should I do?!* But then the mama bear stopped, stood, and sniffed. It seemed the bear wasn't after Brooke because it was still searching. It seemed it was after the . . . birdseed? *Does a bear want seeds meant for tiny birds?* Brooke wondered. Her question was soon answered as the bear used its tongue to pick the seeds off the ground and then stood up and ripped apart the feeder's plastic shell to get to the seeds inside.

The mama bear next turned her attention toward the trash, at which point Brooke finally managed to squeak out a soft, "Bear," to alert her stakeout companions. It was followed by a more robust, "Bear!" which finally woke them. The others jumped up and stuck their heads out of the tent just as the bear knocked over the trash can. They all watched as the bear made its way through the contents and then ambled off into the night.

Mr. Clark jumped out of the tent and, in his bare feet and pajamas and with just a flashlight, tried to follow the bear, but quickly lost its trail.

When he came back, the others had already all spilled out of the tent.

"A bear!" Tai yelled. "I can't believe it. It was a bear!" He turned to Brooke, "That was amazing! How long did you watch it before you woke the rest of us up?"

Brooke stared at him for a moment before finding her voice. "Wow! Did that really just happen?" She told the group about first seeing the bear, thinking it was coming to eat them, and how she hadn't been able to speak.

The group was so amazed they kept talking about the whole event until Brooke said, "Shhhh! I hear something."

The group scrambled back into the tent and peeked out the doorway as a raccoon ambled past on its way to the spilled trash.

"Oh my gosh, it's adorable!" Brooke gushed.

"Hey, look," Izzy whispered, "it has babies."

The group "oohed" and "ahhed" as the raccoon's three kits appeared from behind a tree and followed their mother to the trash. The raccoon family crawled through the trash until most of the scraps were eaten and then moved down the block to the next conveniently tipped-over trash can.

When the raccoons left, the group again poured out of the tent, chattering excitedly. Izzy picked up pieces of the broken bird feeder while Brooke and her dad once again righted the trash can. Tai picked up Blue's bowl but quickly dropped it, yelling, "Gross! It's slimy."

Zack, who had followed Tai over, observed, "I think it's slobber from the bear," making everyone laugh. "Or maybe from a sleuth of bears." Although Zack hardly spoke, he loved the terms for groups of animals.

"Oh, man, this is disgusting," Tai complained.

"So is this," Izzy added, looking at all the spilled garbage.

"Well, team, what we have here is a big mess," Mr. Clark said. "But right now, I think we need to get some sleep. We can clean it up and call the county biologist in the morning."

The kids decided to abandon the tent and camp out in Brooke's basement, where it was cool and quiet. When they finally settled down, Mr. Clark said good night to them and joined his wife in their upstairs bedroom, waking her briefly to tell her about the night's adventures.

8

Brooke thought she was the first one up the next morning, but when she entered the living room wearing her purple polka-dot pajamas, she found her dad in his usual chair.

"Well, good morning, Brooke. Would you like some coffee?" he joked.

"I wish I did today. I feel like I didn't get any sleep last night."

"Try a cold glass of water. Your body probably needs it."

Brooke was dehydrated, and the cold water refreshed her. "Have you been outside yet?" she asked her dad.

"I have," Mr. Clark replied. "I cleaned up the mess and found something I think you kids will find very interesting."

"What is it?"

"Follow me."

Brooke slipped into a pair of sparkly silver flip-flops to follow her dad to the spot where the trash can had stood the night before. There, in the mud at the edge of the driveway, were the raccoon tracks they had already learned about, but they were right next to a different, larger, even more human-like track. In fact, the only thing that told Brooke it wasn't from a human were the prints in front of it from a set of long claws.

"Is that track from the bear?" Brooke asked.

"Exactly. I even looked in Izzy's book to be sure. It's the rear track of a black bear."

"Awesome!" Brooke exclaimed.

Suddenly, the back door squeaked open and Izzy peeked out. "There you are."

"Are the others awake?" Brooke asked.

"Yup."

"Bring them out. My dad found something really cool."

Soon, the whole group spilled into the backyard.

49

"Who cleaned up?" Tai asked.

"My dad," Brooke replied.

"Thanks, Mr. Clark," Tai said.

"Yes, thank you," the others agreed.

Mr. Clark shrugged it off. "I've been up for hours and needed something to do," he said. "I also called the county biologist. She said she'd already received a lot of calls about a bear and will come over this morning to investigate."

"What'd you find that's so cool out here?" Tai asked Mr. Clark.

"Look here," he said and pointed to the bear track. Brooke stepped back so the others could take a look and felt her foot land in something squishy. "Ugh. Not again," she said. They all looked and broke into laughter when they realized she had found the bear's calling card: a big pile of scat. Just then, the biologist pulled up in her truck and they all ran up to greet her. When she got out of the truck, they could see she was tall and fit, with her black hair pulled into a thick braid that almost reached her waist.

"Hello," Mr. Clark said. "Thanks for coming."

"My name's Victoria Perez. Are these your helpers?" she inquired, nodding toward the kids.

"It's sometimes hard to know who's in charge and who's the helper," Mr. Clark laughed. "Come on, I'll show you the damage." He led her into the backyard.

Victoria took a look around. "No wonder you had a bear here," she said. "You have lures all over the place."

"Lures?" Brooke asked.

"Yes, lures. Attractants. You know, things that bring bears in. Not only did you have your trash out all night, you left out a grill dripping with barbecue sauce. I assume there was dog food in this bowl, and there are enough sunflower seed hulls in the grass for me to know there was a bird feeder hanging from this tree. I'm not surprised at all you had a bear come by, and I expect it will come back—especially since it got such a big reward on this visit."

The kids stood with their mouths open.

"Oh, I feel terrible about this," Mr. Clark said. "What can we do to fix the situation?"

"You need to wildlife-proof your house and yard. That means no bird feeders out at night, grills cleaned after use or stored in the garage, pets fed inside, and garbage stored securely until the morning of pickup. And by securely, I don't mean in the garage—bears break into garages. I mean either in your house or in a specially designed, bear-proof storage container."

"Can we leave out the trash cans if we sprinkle pepper on them?" Mr. Clark asked.

"Do you like pepper?" Victoria asked with one eyebrow raised.

"I get your point," Mr. Clark said. "We'll make sure the can is stored securely."

"Great. And one more thing," Victoria added. "No more stakeouts. If a bear or a *mapache*—"

"What's a *mapache*?" Brooke interrupted.

"Sorry—that was Spanish," Victoria laughed. "If a bear or a raccoon comes near any attractant in the future, scare it away *before* it has a chance to get anything. If an animal is rewarded for its efforts, it will want to try again. Not only will the animal come around to your place again and again, but it will seek out the same rewards at other people's homes in the neighborhood."

"It sounds like we did everything wrong!" Brooke lamented. She then muttered to herself, "Or at least I did."

"Most things. But not everything," Victoria said. "Your dad called me, and that was the right thing to do. Now, please get everything cleaned up, and I'll come back tonight with a trap. I need to mark the bear to figure out if it's the same bear getting into trash everywhere in town, multiple bears, or a mix of bears and raccoons."

"All through the town? Do you mean *everywhere* in town?" Tai repeated, trying to remember if he had left any lures out around his own house.

"Everywhere," Victoria said. She pulled out a newspaper article and handed it to Brooke, who was standing nearest to her. "Go ahead, read it," she said.

Brooke stared helplessly at the blurry words. "Let me," Mr. Clark offered, reading aloud over Brooke's shoulder. "Bears continue to ravage trash cans everywhere in town, including ripping into seven garages in the past week." He stopped and said, "It sounds like the bears are a big problem."

"That's the thing," Victoria explained. "People think the bears are the problem, but bears aren't the problem—people are the problem. Bears are drawn into our neighborhoods when they learn people are easy sources of food. People who leave out attractants are the problem."

"People like us," Mr. Clark pointed out.

Victoria nodded.

"People like me," Brooke whispered to herself, her eyes filling with tears.

"Now, if a bear does come back here tonight, keep a good distance from it while yelling to scare it off," Victoria continued to the group.

"Oh, right," Mr. Clark said. "I've read you can

change a bear's behavior by throwing rocks toward it and banging pots and pans to scare it."

Victoria sighed. "Actually, that isn't true. You can do those things to get a bear to leave an area long enough to clean up the attractants, but the only thing that really works is proper storage of food and trash. I can't emphasize it enough: once a bear learns about human food and trash, you can't get it to *un*learn. I'd better get going if I'm going to get back with a trap in time to set it tonight."

As the group thanked Victoria and watched her pull away, Brooke tucked behind a tree to hide her tears from the others.

9

That night, Victoria came back, pulling a big gray metal culvert trap on a trailer behind her truck. Brooke, Izzy, Tai, and their families were all waiting for her to arrive.

Clearly, Victoria was used to onlookers, because she started explaining to everyone what she was doing as soon as she got out of the truck.

"This is a bear trap. It's also called a culvert trap because it's made out of a culvert—the large metal tubes used to allow water to flow under roads—and has doors welded onto each end," Victoria explained while unhooking the trailer. As she expertly leveled the trap, she added, "Most animals like to go up when entering small spaces, but if I set the trap at an angle, the door won't swing closed, so I keep it flat."

She opened the door at one end of the trap,

wired a bag baited with fresh melon juice to a lever, and closed and relocked the door. She then opened the other end and kept it open. Finally, she threw chunks of melon into the trap. "When a bear smells the bait, it will enter here and then follow the trail of melon to the bait bag. The bait bag is attached to the lever that triggers the door to close behind the bear. Hopefully, we will catch the bear and not a raccoon or other animal."

"Does it hurt the bear?" Izzy worried.

"It doesn't hurt the bear, but hopefully it will scare the bear," Victoria answered. "And then maybe the bear will associate coming here with a bad experience and stay away in the future."

"Aren't the melon chunks food rewards?" Brooke asked.

"Yes," Victoria answered. "I realize it seems like a contradiction to everything I just told you, but without any reward, it will be hard to get the bear in the trap."

"Can we try?" Brooke asked.

"Why not?" Victoria answered while picking

the pieces back up.

"What happens after you trap a bear?" Tai asked. "Do you take it back to the forest?"

"Nope," Victoria stated matter-of-factly. "That doesn't work. If you relocate a bear, but don't get rid of the attractants, the bear will come right back. Besides, we don't want to give another community a problem we created, or release a bear into another bear's home range, or put a bear at risk of getting hit by cars when it makes its way back. Bears are great travelers and can find their way back home from long distances."

"What will you do with it?" Mr. Clark asked.

"I'll give it ear tags to identify it and put a GPS collar on it to track where it goes. Then I'll release it and track it with this useful—although somewhat broken—antenna." Victoria held out a GPS collar and an antenna so the group could study them.

"Isn't that clever," Mr. Clark mused.

"Clever and useful," Victoria said. "I'll release any bear we catch right here, but I believe it will leave right away since you will have made sure there are no food rewards available. With the GPS, we will know where it goes."

"So where do you think it'll go?" Tai asked.

"There are a few possibilities. It may be mostly foraging in natural areas and coming into town for added calories, or it may be finding so much food in town that it's simply staying in town. I don't know."

"What about the raccoons?" Mr. Clark asked. "They are clearly getting into trash, too."

"You're right. It's bears and raccoons, and likely other animals, too," Victoria explained. "If we focus on bear-proofing, we will keep all animals out of human food and trash."

"Why is it so much worse now than, say, two months ago?" Mr. Clark asked.

"When bears are hungry, they are especially vulnerable. That may be the case now. Maybe they were eating insects and are ready to switch to berries, but the berries aren't out yet. It can be a big concern in the fall when bears need to fatten up to prepare for winter hibernation. If there's a lag time between the availability of natural foods at that time, bears are even more likely to get into human food or garbage because all they do during that time of year is look for food and eat."

"Then they must need our food, right?" Izzy's mom, Mrs. Philips, asked.

"No. They have plenty of natural food. It's just that our food is much easier to get."

Right. Easier to get because stupid me was too lazy to get up early and take the trash out in the morning, so I left it out all night, Brooke thought. She frowned while picking at another new pimple on her chin.

"What'll happen to the bear—or *bears*?" Tai asked.

"That depends. If enough berries come out and the bear—or bears—go back to eating natural foods, then all is well. If, on the other hand, the bear—or bears—keep looking for human food and damaging property or entering people's homes, then it's a problem. People start requesting special permits that allow them to kill the bears."

"That's awful!" Brooke wailed, tears now streaming down her cheeks. "It's all my fault. The bear could die and it's all my fault!"

"Honey, what are you talking about?" her dad asked, trying to calm her.

"I'm the one who put the trash out overnight. I'm the one who overfilled the birdfeeder. I'm the one who left dog food in Blue's dish. And I'm the one who made a mess of the grill. It's all my fault!" Brooke cried.

She pulled a half-eaten Astro Bar out of her pocket and was about to stuff it in her mouth when Victoria said, "And you also have the ability to fix it."

"Fix it?" Brooke asked, still holding the candy bar near her mouth.

"Yes, fix it," Victoria answered. "You may have been part of the problem, but now you can be part of the solution. Try to understand it from the bear's point of view. For example, why would you eat a candy bar that does nothing good for you?"

Brooke stuffed her hand with the Astro Bar into her pocket and stared at Victoria, her face flushed red.

"I'll tell you why," Victoria continued. "Candy bars are easy to get, easy to eat, taste good, and give you quick energy. But, in the long run, they create nothing but problems for you. After the initial energy runs out, you end up tired, moody, and hungry. Sugar even has negative impacts on your nails and skin. If it was really hard to get that candy bar, you probably would have had something healthy instead and would be better off for it."

Although some of the others shuffled around uncomfortably, Brooke listened carefully.

"I'm confused," Tai said. "What does the bear have to do with Brooke's candy bar?"

"I think I've got it," Brooke said slowly, thinking of her brother's advice. "To make the bear eat natural food, we need to make the human food and trash really, really hard to get.

And I think I got it that the bear's natural food may not be the easiest thing for it to get at times, but it is best for the bear in the long run.

"But it's not enough for us to just put food and trash away at *my* house. We need to get the whole town to do it so we can save the bear—or bears—and the raccoons." Brooke took a deep breath. "I'm ready to be part of the solution," she said to Victoria. "How can I make that happen?"

"I think what you meant to say is, '*We* are ready to be part of the solution. How can *we* make that happen?'" Izzy added, putting her arm around Brooke.

"Right," Tai said, pulling Zack with him to join Brooke and Izzy. "We're the Nature Club, and our job is to learn about nature and then be helpful!"

"You kids are the Nature Club?" Victoria sounded impressed.

They all nodded.

"I read about you in the paper doing the cleanup of Green County Park. Great job. How long have you kids been meeting?"

"We just started the group this summer, but we plan to get a lot done!" Brooke answered, then added, "And we have to, because Izzy and Zack are only here for the summer—they have to go back to Southern California where they moved last fall before school starts back up." She made a dramatically sad face.

"But in the meantime," Mrs. Philips interjected, "we came back for the summer to be near my mom, so they will have many fantastic weeks together."

"It's terrific they are spending part of their vacation time helping out wildlife," Victoria said to Mrs. Philips and the other adults.

"We agree, and we wholeheartedly support their efforts," Mrs. Philips said. Tai's dad and Brooke's parents nodded in agreement.

"Okay. If you kids want to take this on, here's what you need to do. You need to teach the entire community how to store food and trash and get them to take action—right away. I suggest writing an article for the newspaper and organizing a community meeting. If you set up a meeting, I will come and give a presentation."

"We'll do it!" Brooke said, with enthusiastic agreement from the others.

"One more thing," Victoria added. "There are three good reasons to keep your distance from wildlife. The first reason is to stay safe. When animals feel crowded in, they can get scared and act defensively. A second reason is to not tame animals. When wild animals get used to people, they are more likely to spend time near humans and then get into human food or garbage.

"A third reason is that wild animals carry diseases that can make you sick. Raccoons, for example, can carry roundworm—and you don't want that! Use gloves when cleaning up the trash that animals have been in and spray down the can with ammonia—under your parents' supervision, of course. That will reduce the odors that attract wildlife."

Brooke, Izzy, and Tai looked at each other and smiled. "The Nature Club is going to jump into action!" Brooke said excitedly.

"That's right," Izzy said. "We've got this!"

"I love your enthusiasm. See you all in the morning," Victoria said.

After Victoria and the other biologists left, the others said their goodbyes and headed home to get some sleep and dream about what they might see the following day.

10

Late that night, after the great horned owl started hooting to its mate, the mama bear rose from her day bed and stretched. It was time for her evening patrol. After the previous night's success, she was salivating in anticipation for tonight's food rewards.

As usual, she started by standing on her back legs and sniffing the air. When she detected a new scent, she moved her head from side to side to determine its source. It was coming from the same place as the night before, so she started off on the same route.

Since she hadn't yet had any problems foraging in this new area, she prepared to take her cubs. She nudged them awake and clicked at them to follow her. As she traveled, she moved silently and stealthily, although the same couldn't be said for the cubs, who climbed and played as they went.

The mama bear checked each source of food from the previous night: the grill, the tree where the bird feeder had hung, and the curb where the trash can had sat. Strangely, nothing was there. At the curb, the new scent came in strong. She followed it to a large metal cave of sorts. She continued to sniff and examine the metal cave.

Her cubs followed her in and joined her in sniffing all around the entrance and inside. When they were all in the cave together, the mother bear lifted her head and sniffed the sweet-smelling bag at the end of the metal cave. The scent was strong and sweet. She bit into it and pulled back, and then suddenly—*slam!* The metal door banged shut behind them. The mama bear pushed against it as hard as she could, but it wouldn't budge. She bit and clawed at the edges of the cave but, again, nothing happened.

With no other options, she lay down with her cubs and waited, eventually falling asleep.

***

Meanwhile, the raccoon family was waiting for its turn at the big plastic container when its members were startled by the sound of the trap door closing. The mother raccoon waited a bit and then sniffed and explored her way over to where the trash can usually lay. When it wasn't there, she sniffed about again and immediately picked up the strong and unmistakable scent of a nearby bear. It was coming from a large, unknown metal object in the driveway. She quickly led her kits away to the next house, where a different trash can stood full of scraps but upright on the curb. They climbed in and started to eat.

11

The next day, the group reassembled at Brooke's house. Victoria had indeed caught a bear, and everyone wanted to see it. Since it was Saturday, the adults were off work and would come as well.

As each family arrived, Brooke led them through the house and into the backyard, asking them to be as quiet as possible. Victoria arrived early with the two other biologists, Logan and Cameron. There was only time for a quick "hello" before the biologists got to work setting up inside the garage.

Eventually, Victoria came around the garage and gave the group an update. "Well, team, I have good news and bad news," she said.

Everyone leaned forward eagerly.

"First, the good news. We were successful last night in catching a bear. In fact, we were so successful, we caught three bears: a sow, or female, and her two cubs."

Excitement rippled through the group. Brooke asked what everyone was thinking. "Are we going to get to see the cubs?"

"You are," Victoria answered, "and they're beautiful. However, the fact that there are cubs brings me to the bad news. When a mother brings her cubs into developed areas, the cubs are exposed to her bad habits. The cubs will pick up those habits if they learn they can use them to get food. To prevent that, we need to make it impossible for them to get food so they have no temptation to pick up the habits."

"We'll do it," Brooke said determinedly. "We'll teach this whole town to be bear-proof!"

"Yes, we will!" Izzy, Tai, and Zack yelled out at the same time.

Victoria smiled. "That's terrific," she whispered. "Now, along with being excited, we also need to be quiet. Right now, Logan and Cameron are using a long pole with a syringe mounted on the end to drug the bears so they fall asleep. They'll stay asleep for about fifteen minutes—long enough for us to pull them out of the trap, measure them, mark them, and give the mother a radio collar. Then, we will put them back in the trap to keep them safe while they wake back up."

As if on cue, Logan came out of the garage and motioned to Victoria that the bears were all asleep. Victoria instructed the group to move slowly and quietly around to the garage and, once there, where to stand so they could watch safely without getting in the way.

Everyone followed her instructions, although the kids kept elbowing each other and giggling quietly with excitement.

One by one, the biologists pulled the bears out of the trap. They laid each of them out on a big tarp in the garage, side by side.

When they took out the cubs, Brooke couldn't help herself. "They are adorable!" she squealed.

"They really are," Logan agreed quietly. Then,

starting with the cubs, Logan and Cameron took measurements and blood samples from each bear. After that, they attached a plastic orange tag with the number eight to the mother's ear.

"Oh, wow," Brooke whispered to Izzy. "She's got an orange earring now! That's so cool. Let's name her '*Ocho*' because eight is fun to say in Spanish." Izzy gave Brooke a thumbs-up.

Then Izzy whispered, "I wish Miguel was here. He would have loved to see these bears—except he would have called them *osos*." Miguel lived in Nicaragua but was an honorary member of the Nature Club. He and Izzy had been pen pals for over two years, since their teachers had arranged it back in the third grade.

Cameron took the GPS collar and fitted it around the mother's neck. Throughout the process, Logan recorded each bear's vital signs: blood pressure, heart rate, and breathing rate. The last thing to be done was to weigh each bear. The biologists then placed the bears back in the culvert trap to keep them safe until they were fully awake.

As Cameron closed the trap door, you could hear a collective sigh from the group. Victoria then led the group back to the yard, where she explained more about what they did, why they did it, and bears' health.

"It's a healthy group of bears," she started. "The mother weighs one hundred and thirty pounds. The cubs—both boys—are each about fifty pounds, which is healthy for their age and gender. Based on the wear and color of the mother's teeth, I'd say she's about eight years old. The cubs were born this January, as is true of all cubs of the year.

"Now, you probably saw me looking at her claws." The group nodded. "I was checking their condition. If her claws were really worn down, I would say she was possibly responsible for ripping into some of the sheds in town, but they were in perfect shape. Her teeth were in pretty good shape, too.

"What all that means is we don't think she's

responsible for the damage around town. We will know more when we look at her GPS movement data." Again, a collective sigh came from the group. "Now it's time for us to take the bears to a quiet place to wake up. We'll then release them right at the edge of the neighborhood."

While Victoria talked, Logan and Cameron hooked the trailer to the truck. Then the group followed Victoria to join the other biologists. Mr. Clark stepped forward and thanked the three of them on behalf of the group. Brooke also stepped forward. Turning red, she added, "You can count on the Nature Club for the article and the event. We're going to make things right again."

Victoria smiled. "We're counting on it," she responded, as she hopped into the truck and fired up the engine.

Everyone waved as the biologists, bears in tow, drove down the street, around a corner, and out of sight.

12

Still standing in the driveway, the group spent a good half hour buzzing about what had just happened and how adorable the cubs were. Afterward, the kids got to work with their assignments. They moved to Izzy's house because her mother had a computer they could use.

"If we can write the article and submit it today, maybe we can get it in the Sunday newspaper, which has the most readers," Izzy suggested.

"My dad said he got some good pictures we can send in with the article," Brooke offered.

"Great. We also need to advertise Victoria's Bear Aware event," Tai said. "What do you think of the name 'Bear Aware'? I just thought of it."

"It's perfect," Izzy said. "Now, who should do the main part of the writing?" she asked, eyeing Brooke. "Brooke, this was your idea and you like writing. How about you?"

Brooke nodded, for she was daydreaming about saving the cubs they had seen that morning. But when Izzy pushed the laptop toward her, Brooke saw how blurry the words on the screen looked and she panicked, quickly backing out of the job. "I mean, I, um . . . I have to leave after lunch, so it should be one of you to keep the writing consistent," she stammered.

"What do you have to do?" Tai asked.

"I have to take my dad to the doctor," she responded without looking him in the eye. For some reason, she hadn't told her friends about her blurry vision or her eye appointment and surprised herself by telling that little lie, even as it came out of her mouth.

"I love to read, but Tai is definitely the better writer," Izzy said, taking the laptop back from Brooke and pushing it toward Tai.

So Tai took the lead, and as they brainstormed ideas, he typed them up and then turned them into an article. At first it was way too long, but, working together, they cut it down to three hundred and fifty words. It covered everything they wanted to say, but it still needed to be shorter as the paper limited articles to two hundred and fifty words.

Tai groaned, "I need a break. I'm getting hungry-grumpy."

"Me too," Izzy agreed.

Brooke, who had secretly eaten an Astro Bar, had energy from the sugar, but kept it to herself.

Just then, Mrs. Philips called out to them, "Is anyone ready for lunch? Cody is making burritos."

Cody, Mrs. Philips's new boyfriend, had recently become more of a fixture around Izzy's house and although he wasn't much of a cook, he did make good burritos.

"We're all hungry," Izzy replied for the group.

About ten minutes later, Mrs. Philips emerged with a picnic blanket she spread out in the grass.

Cody came out next, carrying a tray with lunch, glasses, and a pitcher of lemonade while pointing and saying, "Red-tailed hawk above the big willow."

"A beauty," Izzy's mom remarked, looking up. Turning her attention to the kids, she asked, "How's the article coming?"

"It's . . . it's okay," Izzy replied cautiously.

"What are you talking about?" Tai teased. "It's great!" Growing more serious, he added, "We could use your help with editing, though, Mrs. Philips. It's too long."

"Sure thing," she responded. "I'll take a look after lunch."

When lunch was over, Brooke reluctantly thanked Mrs. Philips and headed home.

"Don't worry about the article, Brooke. We'll shorten it and send it to the newspaper this afternoon," called out Mrs. Philips.

13

Brooke left the group and slowly walked home so her dad could take her to the eye exam. She wished she could talk to her brother. It seemed like he was the only one who would understand.

When Brooke got into the car with her dad, she was sullen and quiet. She had been on a sugar high and excited about the article, but then she lost all her energy and got grumpy when she had to leave early. Now she was getting upset about the thought of getting glasses. A part of her body was no longer working and never would be the same again! And it wasn't just her eyes. Lately, she was tired and moody all the time, and there always seemed to be a new pimple on her chin.

Mr. Clark, however, was upbeat. "It will be so great for you to see clearly again," he said cheerfully to Brooke.

"You're just assuming I need glasses and I haven't even had the appointment!" Brooke cried.

Mr. Clark sighed and drove the rest of the way in silence.

Waiting for her appointment, Brooke watched two older girls look at frames for glasses. They were studying a special display for "female athletes" and having fun picking out pairs for each other.

Finally, Brooke was called in for her appointment. The optometrist was a short, funny man who put her at ease with corny jokes as he gave her a series of eye tests. Between tests, Brooke looked around his office. It was decorated with photos of smiling children wearing glasses. After about a half hour, the optometrist said he was done and she could now pick out her first pair of frames.

"But . . . ," she started.

"But what?" he asked. "But aren't you lucky to get brand-new glasses so you can see!"

Brooke looked down at her hands and said

quietly, "I guess."

She didn't want to look the optometrist in the eye or continue with this conversation, so she focused on the photos on the wall behind him. "Are those your patients?" she asked.

"Yes," he responded excitedly. "Those are all children who live in Nicaragua. I go there once a year with a load of donated glasses to give them."

"Don't they have optometrists in Nicaragua?"

"Oh, yes, but Nicaragua is a poor country. Many of these kids don't have money for food, let alone glasses. I should know," he added, "because I was one of those kids. When I was seven, I so badly wanted to learn to read, but I needed glasses and my family couldn't afford them. We also didn't have access to healthy food, so I was sick a lot and had constant headaches, making my eyesight even worse."

"You?"

"Oh, yes. That's why I focus on that country, but there are many places where children go without glasses, even here in the United States."

"Really?"

"Yes. And many children in the United States also lack access to healthy food. You know, junk food is often cheaper than healthy food—and more available. If many parents had more of a choice, they would certainly feed their children more vegetables and less junk food so their children would feel better and have healthier bodies. You know, your health affects everything, from your mood to your skin, to your ability to learn and make good decisions." He paused and smiled at Brooke.

"Now, instead of focusing on what's sad in the world, let's focus on what we can do about it. Maybe one day you will donate your glasses for others to use," he suggested enthusiastically.

It was then that she understood what all the photos in his office had in common: they were all of children who had received glasses through donations.

"I will," she replied and took a deep breath. "You're right, I'm very lucky to get new glasses and," she paused, feeling the candy bar wrapper in her pocket, "to have access to healthy food."

Brooke hopped out of her seat and followed the optometrist to find her dad in the waiting room. For the first time that afternoon, she smiled at him. "I'm done. Will you help me pick out my first pair of glasses?"

Mr. Clark helped Brooke pick out a pair of purple, sparkly frames made specifically for female athletes. While they waited for the frames to be fitted with lenses designed for Brooke's eyes, Brooke took a restroom break to toss the Astro Bar from her pocket into the trash.

When the glasses were ready, one of the technicians adjusted them to fit Brooke's face, proclaimed them to be perfect, and congratulated Brooke on her first pair of glasses. Brooke thanked the technician and took a long look at her face in the mirror. She could now see perfectly, and she liked what she saw. Rather than taking away from her sense of style, the glasses enhanced it with their amazing color and funky sparkles.

Out of habit, Brooke and her father stopped for ice cream on the way home. Brooke was about to order a cone when she thought better of it and suggested they get berry smoothies with yogurt instead. Her father agreed, and, as it turned out, they were just as delicious as any ice cream would have been.

14

The article came out on Sunday in the local paper. Both Tai's and Izzy's families logged onto the online version and found the article right away. Brooke's family still got the printed newspaper delivered to their house on Sundays. She came down to find her parents each reading a section of the paper. The local news section, however, was sitting untouched next to her mother.

Brooke hesitantly walked into the room. "Good morning, Brooke," Mr. Clark greeted. "Your mother and I are hoping you will read the local section to us out loud. Or, at least," he paused for effect, "the leading article."

"Really?! We're the leading article?" Brooke responded, her eyes wide under her new purple glasses and her face wearing a huge smile.

"Congratulations!" her mother said, handing

her the paper.

Brooke took it and looked at the article. "I can read it perfectly!" she enthused and read the title, "Got Bears? Together We Can Solve Our Town's Trash Problem If We Act Fast." She looked up to see her parents smiling at her before reading the rest of the article to them.

"Excellent article. I bet you'll get a great turnout at the Bear Aware event on Tuesday," Brooke's mom remarked.

"I hope the high school gym is big enough," Mr. Clark added.

His wife laughed. "Luckily, we live in an awfully small town."

"I have to call Izzy and Tai!" Brooke shouted while running out of the room to find a phone.

When Brooke hung up the phone, she headed to her room for a candy bar to celebrate, but just as she was about to take a bite, she stopped, dropped the candy bar into the trash, and walked out of the room. Then she walked back into the room, took the candy bar out of the trash, covered it with pepper, and dropped it back into the trash. Finally, she walked back into the room, took the candy bar back out of the trash, walked into the kitchen, and sent the candy bar down the garbage disposal. Brooke then took a deep breath and exhaled slowly, saying to herself, "I can do this."

She cut up carrots, celery, and peppers and put them in a bowl in the refrigerator so they would be easy to grab when she wanted a snack. Brooke grabbed an apple, polished her glasses, and sat down to write a long email to her brother about trapping the bears, learning a lot of the problem was her fault, and finding a way to solve it.

15

Two days later, it was time to join Izzy and Tai to set up the Bear Aware event. Brooke put on her Nature Club T-shirt and headed over.

When she got there, Tai, Izzy, and Zack were already there and all wearing their T-shirts, too. They had given themselves two hours to set up, getting started right away by putting up a huge poster at the front door of the school stating, "Tonight's Bear Aware event is sponsored by the Nature Club."

Victoria, Logan, and Cameron also arrived early and set up a bear trap for people to look at, plus a display of the types of things that attract bears to homes, including bird feeders, pet food, and dirty grills.

Mr. Clark, who helped the biologists lay out their display, laughed to himself at how obvious it all seemed now, when, just a week ago, he hadn't known anything about bears or bear attractants. He also put out a donation jar to raise money for a new radio receiver for the biologists.

Logan gave the kids a stack of Bear Aware magnets to hand out to people as they came in. The magnets listed all of the common bear attractants, with a picture of a bear to remind people to keep their homes bear-proof. When Tai looked at them, he said, "Bear Aware . . . I thought I came up with that name."

Logan laughed. "You probably did, but so have many of us. It's pretty catchy," he said.

The kids each put a magnet in his or her pocket to take home before settling in at the front door to wait for people to arrive. It started as a slow trickle, with many of the early arrivals being the same people who came to the river cleanup. As it got closer to start time, it became a flood of people. The room was at full capacity when it was time to begin. Even Izzy's Grandma Pearl had come to learn about bears.

Like at the river cleanup, Tai nudged Izzy, as president, to introduce the event. Turning red, Izzy announced, "Welcome to tonight's Bear Aware event, sponsored by the Nature Club." At that, she had to stop to give the huge crowd a chance to clap and cheer. She continued, "When bears break into our garbage cans and garages, it's easy to get mad at them, but it's not their fault— it's ours. More importantly, we hold the key to solving the problem. Together, we can do it."

Again, Izzy had to stop while the crowd cheered. "Please welcome Biologist Victoria Perez, who will update us on what's happening in our community and what we need to do—right away—to fix it." The crowd clapped and cheered while Izzy sat down, and Victoria took the stage.

"Thank you all for coming here tonight," Victoria began. "Just your presence gives me hope. I'm going to start by talking about bears. Bears are omnivores. They will eat just about anything. They are also curious, learn quickly, and are strong with long claws. Finally, they need to eat a lot—especially before hibernation. For these reasons, they will get into human food and trash if it isn't stored properly."

Victoria had the audience hooked. She talked more about biology, and about what was happening with the flipped trash cans and ripped-up sheds. "But is it one bear that seems to be everywhere or are there multiple bears in town?" she asked the crowd. People looked at each other and shrugged. No one spoke; they were mesmerized.

"Thanks to GPS technology, my colleagues and I can answer this question," announced Victoria, nodding at Logan and Cameron. While she explained how they caught bears and put GPS collars on them, Logan passed a few collars around through the crowd. "This week, we put GPS collars on three bears. One of the bears is an adult female with two cubs, one is a young female without cubs, and the third is a young male.

"As it turns out, the female with cubs is only entering the edge of town, and the other two bears are moving together through the rest of the town. In other words, instead of one bear being everywhere, everywhere we have bears. I suspect the two bears who are moving together are siblings.

"So what does that tell us? It tells us the stakes for not being bear-aware are high. Right now, the adult female is just starting to expose her cubs to human food. If we cut them off now, they may not pick up the behavior. As for the other two, if I'm right and they are siblings, they may have learned the habit from their mother.

"It's also possible they figured it out themselves, but we need to get them to stop right away because they are already old enough to carry this habit for life and even pass it along to their cubs." Victoria went on to give some case studies and take questions.

She closed by saying, "Together, we can make a difference. If everyone removes all the bear attractants from their yards, secures their sheds, and even moves bear attractants like bananas from the windows of their homes, we can make a huge difference. Most importantly, please don't leave trash out overnight. Put your cans by the curb the morning of pickup.

"I've seen lots of berry bushes with ripe berries this week. There is plenty of natural food out there for bears, they just need the incentive to find it. Tonight, I ask all you good people in the audience to sign an agreement on your way out, promising to give bears that incentive before this week's trash pickup. Will you? Only together can we do this!" At that, the audience clapped and gave her a standing ovation.

After the event, a huge line of people formed to sign the agreement and put money in the donation jar. Dozens of people stayed to look at the displays, trade stories, and speak to the biologists. Several people also stopped to thank the Nature Club kids for putting the event together and writing such a nice article.

16

That same day, Ocho foraged with her cubs on the wild raspberries that were becoming ripe just past the edge of town. They used their lips and tongues to pull the berries from the branches, seeming not to mind the thorns at all. Although they weren't far from a road, the bears stayed just deep enough in the bushes that not a single driver noticed them. They foraged until early evening, when they wandered deeper into the forest and settled into a depression in the ground to nap.

They napped in that spot until nightfall, when Ocho rose to patrol the neighborhood. Her movements didn't wake the cubs, so she nudged them awake and chased them up a tree for their own safety. After the previous week's trouble with the strange metal cave, she wasn't going to bring them this time.

As always, she started by sniffing the air. The scents were less tempting tonight, but she followed the path she knew from memory to have food rewards. On this night, however, there were none. No grills, no bird feeders, and no plastic containers. Defeated, she ambled back to her cubs, called them down from the tree, and curled back up with them in a depression in the ground.

She tried again to forage for human food and garbage over the next few nights, but after failing to get anything, she stopped trying. The berries were now fully ripe, and there was no reason to waste time traveling into town for food.

There was enough natural food for her and her cubs to gain enough weight to make it safely through winter.

As for the raccoon and her kits, they had a similar experience. Not only did they not find a trash can conveniently knocked over for them, they didn't even find a trash can. Instead, they returned to searching for earthworms, catching mice, and finding plenty of other natural food away from homes and roads. As such, few humans saw them that week or knew what became of them.

17

The following Saturday, Izzy and Tai were back at the creek, practicing karate and waiting for Brooke. Although they didn't take karate classes during the summer, they wanted to be ready for classes in the fall. They practiced until Brooke finally showed up, eating a carrot, waving a piece of paper, and smiling. She felt healthier and more energetic than she had in weeks.

"Hey, guys!" Brooke called, running over. "We raised enough money to buy a new radio antenna for the biologists! And we even have two hundred dollars to spare. When my dad told Victoria, she said we could donate the extra money to a cause of our choice."

"Oh, wow!" Izzy exclaimed and immediately started thinking of all the wildlife causes needing donations.

"And check this out!" Brooke continued. "My dad printed this article from the morning paper. It's called, 'Community Effort Succeeds.'"

Immediately gaining the others' attention, Brooke read, "On Tuesday night, the Nature Club sponsored a Bear Aware night attended by more than one hundred and fifty members of the community. The event featured educational displays and a talk by Biologist Victoria Perez about bears and how to protect them by keeping our homes bear-proof. At the end of her talk, Perez asked the crowd to sign an agreement stating they would bear-proof their homes before Friday morning's trash pickup. Apparently, everyone did, because on Friday, there were no reported incidents of bears—or raccoons—tipping over trash cans, getting food, or breaking into sheds."

Brooke looked up to see Izzy and Tai grinning from ear to ear and high-fiving each other.

"We did it!" Tai shouted. He looked at Brooke. "And look at you, reading with those purple glasses! They are so cool."

Izzy nodded. "We were so busy on Tuesday, I never even got a good look at you. Those are awesome. Are they real?"

"Actually, they are," Brooke answered.

"Is that why you haven't been reading or writing lately? How come you didn't tell us you needed glasses?" Izzy asked.

"I don't know," Brooke answered. "I think I was scared something about me was changing for the worse. But now I'm just grateful the glasses let me see clearly. I even got to write a long email to my brother this morning without having to squint or make the font huge."

"Seeing's a great thing. So is hearing. Did you know I wear hearing aids?" Tai asked. "I love them—had them since I was a little kid."

"No kidding? I didn't know that," Brooke said. "Then I'm also grateful the hearing aids let you hear clearly! I guess I was being a little bit ridiculous."

"No way," Tai said. "I hated them at first. My

dad says I'd take them out and hide them under my bed. Then one day my dad tricked me. He said, 'Tai, the ice cream truck is going to drive down our street today. If you tell me when you hear it, I'll buy you some ice cream, so you need to wear your hearing aids.' I said, 'Dad, I can hear that truck even without my hearing aids.' Then he said, 'Have you heard it yet today? Because it's already been down the street three times.' I hadn't, so I put in those hearing aids, and by the end of that day, I got my ice cream. I believe I've worn them every day since my dad's trick—and boy, have they been great."

"How was that a trick?" Brooke asked.

"My dad had asked the driver to turn the music way down to be sure I wouldn't hear it without those hearing aids because, the truth is, ice cream trucks make more noise than a squealing hog. Anyway, you just have to get used to them."

"I think I'm already used to them. I'm even starting to really like them," Brooke admitted.

"They are perfect for you! I want a pair like

that!" Izzy exclaimed.

"Me too, except with way more sparkles," Tai teased.

They laughed and then Brooke got serious. "My optometrist grew up in Nicaragua," she said.

"Like my pen pal, Miguel!" Izzy exclaimed.

Brooke nodded. "He told me a lot of kids in Nicaragua struggle with poverty. He collects glasses for them and will even send mine down when I'm done with them."

"That's terrific," said Izzy. "I'll send a letter to Miguel to tell him!"

"The thing is," said Brooke, "the optometrist said it isn't just in Nicaragua. He said there are children all over the world who need glasses, even in the United States. And glasses are only part of it. There are kids in our community who don't even have enough food."

"That's just not right," Tai said.

"My mom says when people are in need, the most important thing isn't that you do the *perfect* thing, but that you do *something*," Izzy suggested.

"That doesn't make sense," said Tai. "What if you donate socks when someone needs food?"

"I think she meant that doing *some*thing is better than doing nothing," Izzy said, "assuming that the something is helpful."

"Sort of like how we didn't pick up trash across our whole town, but we sure made a difference at Green County Park?" Tai said.

Izzy nodded.

"Let's donate that extra money to the local food bank," Tai said. "I can't stand to think of hungry kids in our own neighborhood."

"But aren't we the Nature Club?" Izzy asked, "and didn't we raise the money to save bears—or at least animals?"

Brooke thought about it for a moment. "Humans are animals," she said. "We spent a lot of money on bears, and Victoria said we can spend the rest on whatever cause we want. I want to spend the rest on human animals."

"Okay. I'm in!" Izzy said. "It makes sense and

it's the right thing to do."

"I'll ask my dad to make the donation and let Victoria know," Brooke said. "I think we should ask them to spend all the money on fresh fruit and vegetables for the kids. The kids will be healthier for it and feel better, too. I should know," Brooke smiled proudly. "I gave up eating Astro Bars, and I feel better already."

"Awesome!" Izzy responded. Then only half-teasing, she added, "I thought you seemed happier."

"Thanks," replied Brooke sincerely. "I believe in myself and think I can do it, but I will need the support of my friends to keep me on track."

"How about if I support you by eating the extras?" Tai suggested.

"Sorry. I made them disappear," answered Brooke. "And, really, the best way to support me is if we all eat healthy together."

"I'm in," Tai said.

"Me too," Izzy added. "I pinky promise," she added, linking her pinky around Brooke's. "Then

Izzy wondered aloud, "Should we change our name to the Nature and People Club?"

This time Tai got to laugh, "Since people are in the animal kingdom, I think we're covered."

"I'm glad we're doing something to make a difference," sighed Brooke.

"I agree," Tai said. "What should we do next?"

"One step at a time," Izzy interjected. "For today, let's celebrate bears: wild, wonderful bears. Tomorrow we can plan our next move."

"Agreed," said Tai with a big grin, and the three friends pulled out their water bottles to prepare for a toast.

"To nature!" said Izzy.

"And wildness!" said Brooke.

"And bears!" said Tai.

They all took long drinks and spent the rest of the day sketching in their journals and playing at the creek until it was time to go. Then, before leaving, they spent five minutes together looking for trash, and for the first time in as long as they could remember, they couldn't find any.

Notes on Black Bears

by Brooke Clark

American black bears, called *Ursus americanus* in Latin, are the smallest of the three types of bear that live in the United States, and they are the ones with the widest range. The others are polar bears (only found in Alaska) and grizzly, or brown, bears (only found in Alaska, Wyoming,

Montana, Idaho, and occasionally Washington). Black bears are found in forty-one of the fifty states.

Black bears have round, heavy bodies with short, fuzzy tails. (Cute!) Their thick fur can be black, brown, cinnamon, or blonde. They don't have shoulder humps like grizzlies; their face has a straight profile; and they have short, curved claws and tall, pointed ears. When you see a bear's profile, its head is lower than its rear.

Black bear tracks are easy to identify. The back ones look like human tracks. The main differences are that in bear tracks, the outside toe is the biggest (the opposite of a human track) and claw marks usually show. The front tracks also look like human tracks, except they either don't show the heel or show just a little print that's separate from the palm part.

Black bears are classified as carnivores but are actually omnivores. They eat plants, berries, seeds, acorns, insects, fish, and even small animals like fawns!

During winter hibernation, black bears won't eat for up to four months. (I can't imagine!) To prepare, they spend autumn fattening up. That means eating a lot of food quickly. Bears are perfectly adapted to do this, since they are curious, have excellent senses of smell, and are strong with sharp teeth and claws.

Unfortunately, these same adaptations get bears in trouble with people. Once bears learn that humans are a source of high-calorie food, they can't unlearn it and will just keep looking for human food. Bears will even switch from being diurnal (day-active) to being nocturnal (night-active) if it gives them access to human food.

When bears try to get human food, they get into trouble with humans. The only way to fix it is to make sure bears never get a taste of human food or trash.

The most important thing you can do to keep bears wild is to properly store all food and trash at all times. Food includes pet food, garbage, sweet hay for horses, and bird feeders. It is also important to remove anything else that might attract bears to your house. A common example is that it's important to remove fruit from trees as soon as possible.

Notes on Raccoons

by Brooke Clark

Raccoons, called *Procyon lotor* in Latin, are medium-sized mammals that are known for their stylish black-and-white face masks and striped tails. They are good swimmers and climbers, and they can rotate their feet backward to move straight down a tree or other surface!

Raccoon tracks have long toe marks and can be up to four inches long. The back tracks have longer heel marks than the front tracks. Sometimes, the claw marks even show.

In North America, raccoons can live all the way from Canada to Panama. They are really adaptable. They are found in all kinds of habitats and can sleep and have their litters in anything from tree hollows to rock crevices to crawl spaces in buildings.

Raccoons are famous for wetting their food before they eat it. Everyone used to think they wet it to wash their food or to make it easier to swallow. Scientists now think they are actually wetting their paws to increase their sensitivity.

Like black bears, raccoons are omnivores, but they eat an even crazier range of food, from earthworms to birds' eggs, to acorns, to fish.

Like bears, raccoons fatten up in the fall to prepare for hibernation. Also, like bears, raccoons will change the times they are active to take advantage of human food, but, unlike bears, the time they are normally active is at night.

Most importantly, the only way to keep raccoons wild is the same as with bears—it's by keeping all food and garbage stored at all times.

If you see a raccoon, don't approach it. Raccoons can bite and scratch humans and carry diseases that humans can get.

Questions to Consider:

1. When Brooke learns she needs glasses, how does she react?

2. What were some similarities and differences between the way the raccoons searched for food and the way the bears searched for food?

3. Why was Victoria upset that the Clarks left garbage out to lure in wildlife? What could they have done instead to find the culprit?

4. It is hard for Brooke to stop eating candy bars. How does she finally succeed in giving up the habit?

5. How did Brooke's friends react when they saw her new glasses? How do you think that made her feel?

Join the Nature Club
for more adventures!

www.natureclubbooks.com

Read on for a peek at Book 4 . . .

Making a Splash
Chapter 1

Zack stood below an old willow tree in the backyard and stared at a hole high on the trunk. He had seen a woodpecker carry food to the hole enough times to know she had a nest in there. But to see the nest, he needed to peer into the hole, and to peer into the hole, he needed to climb the tree, and to climb the tree, he needed to hoist himself up onto the lowest branch—but the lowest branch was way above his head. He tried taking a running jump to reach it, but it was just too high.

Determined to see the nest, he went to the shed to get a ladder. The only one he could find was the old wooden one his mom had warned him not to use. He couldn't think of any other way to get high enough to peer into the hole, so he dragged the ladder over to the tree and leaned it against the trunk. Zack climbed up to the fourth rung and then stopped—the wood on the fifth rung was starting to split.

Zack tried to peer into the hole from where he stood, but he was too low. He even got up on his toes, but he was still too low. Slowly and carefully, he set his right foot onto the fifth rung and tested it—it felt stable. He put his weight on it and lifted his other foot up toward the lowest branch when . . . *craaack*! The rung broke and Zack crashed to the ground.

He yelled out as he fell, but when he hit the ground, the air was knocked out of him, and he lay quiet. At first, he wondered if he was still alive, but then he felt a sharp pain coming from his left arm. Yup. He was alive. He lifted his head to look at his arm and saw it was bent at an odd angle between his wrist and elbow. Feeling a mix of pain, nausea, and panic, he yelled, "IZZY!" before laying his head back down.

Izzy, who was sitting on the back porch reading, heard her little brother yell for help, followed by a crash. She threw down her book and ran toward Zack's voice, finding him at the base of the old willow tree. In stark contrast to his bright red hair, Zack's face looked pale and afraid.

"I think it's broken," Zack said in a daze.

"It sure is," Izzy agreed, looking at the broken ladder on the ground next to him.

"No, Izzy, not the ladder. I mean, yes the ladder, but . . . my arm," Zack winced.

Izzy knelt down next to her brother and put a hand on his shoulder. "Don't move, Zack," she said, her voice shaking. "I'm going to get mom."

"Wait, don't leave me," Zack cried, but Izzy was already running to the house.

Izzy opened the back door to yell into the house, "Mom! Hurry!" she yelled. "Zack fell out of the old willow tree and broke his arm."

In moments, Izzy's mom, Scarlet Philips, burst out of the house and raced past her. Cody, Mrs. Philips's friend-who-was-quickly-becoming-a-boyfriend, followed closely behind. Together, they found Zack lying under the tree and moaning softly.

Mrs. Philips took one look at Zack and gasped.

She kneeled at his side and yelled, "Izzy, call Mrs. Clark and ask her to come right away!" Mrs. Clark lived right down the street and worked as an emergency room nurse.

Mrs. Clark arrived within minutes and went straight to Zack. Brooke, Mrs. Clark's daughter, had tagged along and stood by Izzy to watch. The two girls differed both in personality and in style—Izzy was quieter, wore plain outfits, and tied her straight, long brown hair back in a ponytail while Brooke had wild, curly hair and loved to dress in bold, brightly colored outfits but the girls were best friends. They spent so much time with each other that Zack was like a brother to Brooke, and she wanted to make sure he was okay, too.

"Can you describe what happened and tell me what hurts?" Mrs. Clark asked Zack while looking into his eyes and then checking his pulse and breathing.

"I was climbing the ladder, trying to see into the woodpecker hole. I was being careful, but . . .

then the ladder broke," Zack described slowly.

"Did you get a look at her nestlings?" Cody, who had taught Zack much of what he knew about birds, asked.

Mrs. Philips frowned at Cody and said, "How can you worry about seeing baby birds when his arm looks broken and he could have a concussion—or worse?"

Cody looked at Zack and realized he was pale and shaking. Cody kneeled down to put a hand on his shoulder. "You're right, I guess I am a little overly bird-centric," Cody said. He then looked at Mrs. Clark and asked, "How is he?"

Mrs. Clark looked up from assessing Zack's injuries and smiled reassuringly at Scarlet and Cody. "The good news is, I don't believe he injured his head or back, but he certainly does have a broken arm."

Mrs. Philips let out a deep breath. "Thank you so much, Nicole."

"Of course! He doesn't need an ambulance. As soon as I'm done stabilizing his arm, you can drive him to the hospital. If you want, I can drive with you, or watch Carson."

Izzy and Zack's little brother Carson was still a toddler and was napping inside, oblivious to all the commotion.

"Actually, if you could take both Carson *and* Izzy to your house, I'd really appreciate it."

"But Mom," Izzy said. "I want to go to the hospital with you!"

"Oh honey," Mrs. Philips said, "You'd have so much more fun at Brooke's house."

"What if Zack needs me?"

"Come on, Izzy," Brooke urged, pulling on Izzy's arm. "We can make popcorn and watch movies and you can sleep over!"

"Wait," Zack said, suddenly perking up from his daze. "You're going to watch movies and eat popcorn while I go to the hospital? That's not fair. I want to watch movies, too!"

"Hmm. He seems to be doing better already," Izzy noted with a laugh. "And watching movies does sound pretty good. But Mom, will you call me every fifteen minutes with an update?"

"I'll keep you updated every few hours," Mrs. Philips promised. "Unfortunately, hospital visits tend to be very slow. We might be there all night waiting for Zack to get his arm set in a cast."

"A cast? I can't have a cast! I need my arm for the Green County swim-a-thon next week! The Nature Club needs me!" Zack cried.

Mrs. Philips knew how much Zack loved being part of the Nature Club. Izzy, Zack, Brooke, and their friend Tai had formed the club earlier that summer. The goals of the club were to learn about nature and to take action to protect it. Izzy's pen pal in Nicaragua, Miguel, was even a member from afar.

Mrs. Philips also knew how excited Zack was about the swim-a-thon. Izzy, Zack, Brooke, and Tai had entered the Nature Club as one of the five, four-person teams participating to raise money for their favorite cause: Green County Park.

"Zack, I'm so sorry. Maybe Izzy could take over your pledges and apply them to her laps."

"But Mom, it's a team event. Each pledge already applies to everyone on the team's laps added together—not just to the laps of the person who collected that pledge. They need my laps. I'm going to let everyone down!"

Zack, who hadn't cried throughout the whole ordeal of breaking his arm, now broke down sobbing. Izzy brought Zack his favorite stuffed penguin to try and cheer him up while Mrs. Clark stabilized his arm and his mother went inside to prepare an overnight bag. When she returned, Cody carried Zack to the car and they set off to the hospital.

to be continued . . .

Acknowledgments

I am grateful to Wren Sturdevant, Max Sturdevant, John Sturdevant, Elettra Cudignotto, Rachelle Dyer, Allan Mazur, Polly Mazur, Sophie Phillipson, Spencer Phillipson, Kelly Phillipson, Julie Tribe, Matthew Tribe, Lisa Rhudy, Michael Ross, Jennie Goutet, Chuck Carter, Jenny Mahon, Leslie Paladino, Jessica Santina, and Sarah Hoggatt, for their help and encouragement.

I am also grateful to Carl Lackey, bear biologist at the Nevada Department of Wildlife, who generously provided expert review.

About the Author

Rachel Mazur, Ph.D., is the author of *Speaking of Bears* (Globe Pequot, 2015), the award-winning picture book *If You Were a Bear* (Sequoia Natural History Association, 2008), and many articles for scientific and trade publications. She is passionate about writing stories to connect kids with nature—and inspiring them to protect it. Rachel lives with her husband and two children in El Portal, California, where she oversees the wildlife program at Yosemite National Park.

To learn more about The Nature Club series, please visit natureclubbooks.com.

To learn more about the art of Elettra Cudignotto, please visit elettracudignotto.com.

To learn more about the art of Rachelle Dyer, please visit rachellepaintings.com.

Made in the USA
Las Vegas, NV
19 March 2021